ISBN 978-0-483-83005-9
PIBN 10073303

Clontarf

An Irish National Drama
In Four Acts.

— BY —

Rev. J. B. DOLLARD, P.P., Litt.D.

Author of

Irish Mist and Sunshine, The Gaels of Moondharrig, Irish Lyrics and Ballads, Collected Poems of Father Dollard, The Jesuit Trail and other Poems of New France, etc.

baile áta cliat.

DUBLIN:

comluct na firinne catoilice i néirinn,
CATHOLIC TRUTH SOCIETY OF IRELAND,

24 Spáid Uac. Uí Conaill.
24 Upper O'Connell Street.

Athlone Printing Works Co. Ltd.

THIS Play of *Clontarf* is dedicated to the people of Ireland as a National Drama, for, in spite of all that has been said to the contrary, the Irish people constitute a Nation to-day and have always constituted a Nation. Under their own " High Kings " in the past they were even a formidable military Nation.

The year of Clontarf marks, perhaps, the most glorious epoch, from a material point of view at least, of all Ireland's history. The crushing of the Danes was an achievement that no other race in the world at that time could accomplish, and therefore Clontarf should forever be an inspiration to Irishmen in all times of trial or of great national peril. The material for this Play has been taken from the Irish accounts in *The Wars of the Gael and The Gall*," and from the Danish narrative in the Sagas, especially in the great Icelandic Saga of Burnt Njal. One of the most dramatic episodes in all history is that of the taking of Thorstein, Son of Hall, at Clontarf, where he scorned to fly with the rest of the Danes.

" What is the use of running ? " he asked with sublime naiveté, " I could not get home to-night anyway, for I am at home out in Iceland ! " And the Irish chieftain magnanimously spared his life, which is more than Achilles or Ajax would have done in like circumstances.

In the matter of fighting prowess there seems to have been a great deal of mutual respect between the Irish warriors and their Viking foes. When Ireland is a free nation once more, one of her great artists will some day paint a masterpiece. He will depict the battlefield of Cluain-Tarbh.

In the background will be seen glimpses of Ben
Edair, and the blue Irish Sea with lines of high-
prowed Viking galleys tossing thereon. Great
masses of Norsemen will be seen fleeing, with
blanched and terrified faces, before the bloody
axes of the Dalcassians. In the foreground a
gigantic young Viking, yellow-haired and blue-
eyed, resting on one knee will look up defiantly
at the terrible, gore-splashed figure of Kerthialfad,
in whose face astonishment and admiration will
be shown. Underneath the picture this title
will appear :—

> " Kerthialfad, son of Malachi, and foster son
> of King Brian, giving Peace to Thorstein, son
> of Hall of the Side, the Bravest of the Brave."

All honour to the Vikings! Men of blood
indeed they were, but never of treachery or the
poisoned bowl. They fought their last great
fight at Clontarf, a battle-royal whose din and
slaughter affrighted a timid and cowering world.
Their raven-bannered, chimera-peaked galleys
have long ceased to haunt the hyperborean seas.
The fitful lights and colours of the aurora shall
nevermore tinge their bulging sails and crackling
pennants. The wild spirits of the Sea Kings,
up-borne by compassionate Valkyries, have
entered into the eternal Halls of Valhalla ; but
the wintry surges lashing the wolf-toothed crags
of Faroe and the Orkneys, still chant for them
in hollow caves a hoarse and mournful requiem.

The Vikings in their Sagas seem to have
made it a point never to under-rate their foes,
and they give full credit to the Irish Chiefs for
their valour and to the Irish army for its victory.

Neither have I, in this play, denied the courage
of the Sea Kings ; rather have I given their
good qualities an unusual prominence. In
" Clontarf " I have kept close to history and
tradition, and have endeavoured to avoid obscur-

ing the text by an attempt at "fine writing"
or poetic figures. Almost the only figures I
have used are the naive, yet strong similes I
have found in the Irish or Danish versions, and
they are, after all, the most suitable for the time
and the circumstances. I have tried to make
it a real Irish drama, expressing the true national
and religious feeling of the Gaelic Race, and not
tinged with pagan thought and feeling or with
modern decadence, like some other plays written
in our time. In this spirit "Clontarf" is offered
to the Irish People, and it is now their privilege
to welcome or reject it.

Toronto, Canada, January 10th, 1920.

CLONTARF.

A DRAMA.

DRAMATIS PERSONÆ.

King Brian, Ard Righ of Ireland
Gormly, his queen
Mailmora, Prince of Leinster
Prince Murrough, son of Brian
Prince Donough, son of Brian
Kerthial, a chief, foster son of Brian
Melmary, King of Hy Liathan
Fridolin, a Bishop
MacLiag, the King's Harper
Laiten, a Herald
Prince Thorstein, Son of Hall, of Iceland
Earl Sigurd of the Orkneys
King Sitric of Dublin
Flosi ⎫
Kari ⎪
Gunnar ⎪
Asmund The White ⎬ Vikings.
Hrafn, The Red ⎪
Erling of Straumay ⎪
Ospak ⎪
Brodar ⎭
Princess Reinalt, Daughter of Murrough
Nuala, her handmaiden
Soldiers, Danes, Attendants, etc.

CLONTARF.

A DRAMA..

Act I—Scene I.

[*A room in King Brian's Palace at Kincora.
Gormly, the faithless wife of Brian, who is secretly
in league with the Danes, is speaking with her
brother, Mailmora, Prince of Leinster, a tributary
of King Brian. He kisses her hand.*]

Mailmora :—
　　God save thee, royal sister !
Gormly :—
　　So thou'rt come
　　To make obeisance for thy vassalage,
　　And in thy person make proud Leinster cringe
　　Unto Momonia's king. · What tribute now
　　Across the plains and mountains have ye
　　　borne
　　To please the usurper Brian ?
Mailmora :—
　　Three great masts
　　From the renowned forests of Imayle
　　For Brian's warships we have carried here.
　　Long was the strain, and all went passing well,
　　Until we neared the palace, when the men—
　　Of different tribes they were—who bore the
　　　masts,
　　Began disputing who should enter first
　　The royal dun. To settle the dispute
　　I put my shoulder to the tree up-borne
　　By the Hy-Phaelan clan, to signify

They had first right ; but as I stepped away
A broken bough caught at my royal sash
And tore it thus.   Fair sister, would'st thou
   mend
The ugly rent ?—I had it from the King.
Gormly :—
Let's see then—Take it off—a goodly sash !
With Brian's household mark upon it worked;
Why 'tis thy *Taurcrec !* Tis the sign thou
   wear'st
That thou art subject to him.   But for this
Thou wert indeed an independent king
And worthy noble Laighean.   What a shame
To wear the mark and livery of a slave,
Whose fathers bent the knee to none on earth!
Art brother mine, or but a base-born kern ?
Yea, I shall mend it—Rather I shall mar.
[*She goes over to the fireplace, and casts the sash
therein to burn.*]
Mailmora :—
I shall not dare appear before the King
His eyes are like an eagle's.   He will miss
His scarf of honour.
Gormly :—
Rather say his scarf of shame and bondage:
   Art thou not a king
Of Leinster's royal blood ?
Mailmora :—
'Tis true I am,
Yet not the lawful filler of the throne.
Did not King Brian at thine own request
Dethrone the rightful ruler and confer
The throne on me ?   Why should I grudge
   him   then
A petty tribute ?
Gormly :—
Hear the ignoble fool !
Art thou a base-born slave, I ask again,
That in thee stirs no aspiration high
For lordship over all of Erin's land ?

But do my will, and I will make thee yet
Ard Righ in Erin.   Look thou, I am sick
Of this too pious monarch and his prayers
And solemn chantings.   The old Pagan strain
Within my blood calls out unto its own.
I will go back to Sitric—my own son
By Olaf of the Sandal ; he is King
Of all the Danes of Dublin.   Him I'll send
Far thro' the Northern seas to gather swift
The galleys of the Vikings,   They shall break
The haughty crest of Brian, whom I loathe
Because in spite of my entreaties
He keeps thee subject.   I will leave him now
And when thy clansmen turn them Leinster-
   wards
I will be one amongst them.   Then to Dublin
To set the blooded Vikings on their prey.
Ha ! 'twill be royal sport, and worthy me,
Who oft before with kings and kingdoms
   played !
Mailmora :—
Well, be it as thou sayest, royal sister,
Thou wilt not be gainsaid, but much I fear
The upshot of this quarrel with great Brian ;·
For he is great indeed, and soon may crush
Even the Vikings in their hour of pride.
What then shall happen us ?
Gormly :—
Faint hearted ever !
But go, we must not be discovered here !

·· SCENE II.

*[The great military hall at Kincora. Its high
walls are hung with shields, axes and spears.
Skins of wild beasts are spread upon the floor.
and soldiers of the Dalcassian Battalion are
standing around in groups.*

*In the foreground, seated at a table playing
chess, are Prince Murrough, son of Brian, and*

Conaing an officer. The gigantic young hero, Kerthial, a foster son of the King, is close by, looking at the game. The players make a few moves, then Kerthial speaks, addressing Murrough.]

Kerthial :—

Thou wert a leader on Glenmama's day
While I, alas, lay sick and sad at home ;
Tell us how went the fray, and did the Dane
Show courage ?

Murrough :—

Courage ? My boy, the Vikings never quail
Till all be lost.   We fought them all day long
And when at last they broke, I tell thee, son,
The Glenvigeha vale was matted thick
With dead and dying ! Leinster's troops
   were there
Under Mailmora—them we drove to flight
With equal slaughter.

Kerthial :—

Did the Leinster Prince
Show himself worthy of his noble sires ?

Murrough (laughing) :—

‘ Mailmora, who is now our honoured guest
Fought well ; but, if I say the very truth,
He ran well, too.   He took wings like a bird
And when we followed fast, five leagues away
I found him—like a bird—established high
Among the thick-spread branches of a yew.
We took him prisoner, and spared his life,
I fear to little good.   Lo, here he comes
Of whom we speak.

[Enter Mailmora, ungreeted. The game of chess proceeds, and he stands by, looking on. Murrough becomes perplexed about a certain move, and appears unable to decide. Mailmora stoops and whispers to him, and Murrough makes the suggested move. The game progresses quickly. Suddenly, Conaing gives a cry of triumph, and makes a move that wins the game. Prince Murrough looks darkly at Mailmora, and speaks.]

Murrough :—
   I might have known the game could not be
   won
   Upon advice of yours. 'Twas you that gave
   The Danes advice by which they fought and
   lost
   Glenmama's day. I am but right repaid.
Mailmora :—
   What! am I thus insulted to my face?
[Raising his voice]—
   I tell you, and let all be witness here
   When next I give the Danes a like advice
   They shall not fail, but they and I shall crush
   King Brian's upstart pride. Farewell, till
      then! (*Rushes out*).
Kerthial :—
   Now, by St. Bride, he doth not courage lack
   To beard us thus! What proper insolence!
   But hither comes his Majesty, the King.
[Enter King Brian with attendant. All stand up]
King Brian :—
   Hail chiefs and soldiers; may the peace of God
   And of the spotless Virgin dwell with ye!
   Where is the Prince of Leinster? I was told
   That I should find him here.
Kerthial :—
   Your Majesty,
   He left the hall in hot and angry mood,
   A moment hence, when someone taunted him
   With the advice he gave unto the Danes
   Upon Glenmama's day. And as he went
   He threatened that next time his good advice
   Unto the pirates would have more effect
King Brian :—
   What foolish broils—more fit for smooth-
     faced boys
   Than warriors grown!
        [To attendant.]
   Run quick and bring him back!
   'Twere shame to treat a guest in such a style.

[*The attendant rushes out.   The warriors resume
their play, and the King stands thoughtfully
looking on.   After some time, a noise is heard
outside, and two soldiers enter, bearing the King's
messenger between them.   The messenger is un-
conscious, and the blood is flowing from a wound
in his forehead.*]

King Brian (sternly) :—

What do I see ? How did this outrage come
Unto the High King's servant ? He shall die
Who did this deed, I swear, e'en though he be
My very flesh and blood !

Soldier :—

Your messenger
Great King, o'ertook the Prince of Leinster
    where
The Bridge of Planks the Shannon River
    spans.
He parleyed with Mailmora, who, in wrath,
Struck with a heavy staff most cruelly
And felled the youth to earth ! The Prince
    at once
Put spurs to steed, and galloped fast away
To join his troop.   We saw the coward deed
And quickly carried here the wounded page.

King Brian :—

Ye have done well, and shall have meet
    reward.
Call in the King's best leeches, let them heal
This faithful youth.
                    [*Kerthial salutes*].

Kerthial :—

Your pardon, mighty lord !
Shall I ride after with my company,
And capture this false prince or give him death
With all his band, before the sun has set ?

King Brian :—

No, let him go ; our hospitable laws
Will not permit he comes to hurt or harm
Within our territory.   For the crime

He shall give reason in the proper time,
Aye, even at his palace gates—for now
There rests no arbiter but ruthless war !

SCENE III.

[*The throne room at Kincora. The High
King is seated upon the throne. On his right
hand, a little below, is seated his Bard, MacLiag,
harp in hand, and at the harper's feet two great
Irish wolfhounds are lying. On various seats
around are Fridolin, Bishop of Thomond, Murrough
and Donough, sons of the King, Torlough, son of
Murrough, Kerthial, foster son of Brian, and some
tributary sovereigns—Mothla, King of the Decies ;
Melmary, King of Hy Liathan ; and O'Kelly,
King of Hy Manie.*]
King Brian :—
Princes and chieftains, I have called you here
To settle with you some affairs of State
That need our deep attention. It hath come
Unto our ears that the bold race accursed
Of pagan Lochlann meditate a raid
Of more than common purpose on our shores.
Strange stirrings have been noticed on the
        seas,
And round the northern Isles their crowding
        sails
Flit here and there, like carrion birds a-wing
Croaking for slaughter. Wherefore it seems
        best
That all our captains should prepare for war,
Mustering by the Bridge of Planks in haste
Their kerne and galloglas a week from now.
There let them train in every valiant feat
The famed Dalcassian legions and the strong
And fearless tribes of the Eugenian line.
And you, my brother princes, it seems well
Ye should depart to your respective realms
And bring your chosen men to meet us here.

Melmary :—
> High King, to whom our fealty is pledged,
> We are well-pleased to hear the vigorous word
> You speak to-day. It shall be as you wish.
> Our armies will be here at your command
> Without delay. We hope your Majesty
> Has inkling where the foe intends to land ;
> For that is all-important.

King Brian :—
> Noble Prince,
> Your point is proper ; It is paramount
> That we should know the place where they
>   debark,
> And concentrate our joined forces there ;
> And this is knowledge that I long have sought,
> But to the present without much success.
> In this uncertainty we must recur
> To God for aid, and I will have proclaimed
> Immediate prayer over all the land.
> The Christ for Whose dominion we fight
> Will hear and help us—Hark ! what din
>   is this ?

[*Sounds of loud voices outside. Then two of
the palace guards appear, escorting a noble-looking
Viking in full armour. The Viking is unarmed,
and the guards are holding him firmly.*]

Guards (saluting) :—
> Most potent King, while pacing at the gate,
> We were accosted by this Viking Chief
> Who tried to force his way across us, armed,
> Crying that he had business with the King
> That would not keep. He scarce could be
>   convinced
> That armed strangers could not see the
>   King,
> And, strong protesting, gave up sword and
>   shield.

King Brian :—
> This is, in sooth, a matter very strange.
> Unhand him, men, and let the stranger speak.

Viking :—
    Most Christian King, I here present myself
    As one, who, weary of all pagan gods,
    Would follow Christ. A light hath come
        from Heaven
    Into my sinful and unworthy soul ;
    Long have I worshipped foul and monstrous
        gods,
    'But now no more.

King Brian :—
    Welcome art thou O friend
    Who come'st in armour of our enemy.
    Thou seekest baptism ; our prelate here
    Shall give thee meet instruction, and outpour
    The holy waters on thy pagan head.
    But now from the beginning tell us tale
    Of whom thou art, and what the prodigies
    That have befallen to have stirred thy soul
    To such desire of Christ and of His word.

Viking :—
    My name is Ospak, and I have been called
    Wisest of pagans. With ten ships I lay
    Within a harbour of the Isle of Man,
    And close outside my anchorage were laid
    My brother's twenty ships—Brodar his name
    A Christian and a deacon he had been,
    But has apostatized, and has become
    Cruel as bird of prey. Full tall is he
    And strong of body, and his long, black hair
    Hangs down below his body-belt, in which
    He tucks its ends. One day he came to me
    With story that a royal messenger,
    Sitric, the King of Dublin, had been there
    To ask assistance for a general war
    By all the Vikings 'gainst the Irish king,
    And he had promised aid. He soon would
      sail
    For Dublin with his company entire,
    And urged me too to go. I told him then
    I would not fight a king as good as Brian ;

And dark with anger Brodar left my ship.
That night dread portents - hovered o'er
   his fleet.
And boiling blood so fell upon each deck
That many men were scalded, and at dawn
A man lay dead on every fated ship !
The second night a fearful din arose
And in the air were war-like weapons seen
That pressed and wounded many, and at
   morn
Another man lay dead on every ship !
The third night came the same wild din once
   more,
And ravens with strong claws, and iron beaks,
Attacked till dawn.   Through all that weary
   night
The men of Brodar fought the ravens off
With sword and shield.   But in the morning's
   light
They saw one dead in every deck again,
And fear shook all.   Then Brodar, with
   much pain
Came to my ship and asked me what I
   thought
Of all these portents, and I prayed to Christ.
For light, since by this time I had lost faith
In Thor and Odin ;   then I answered thus :—
"That blood that came in showers means that
   ye
Shall shed much blood full soon—both of
   your own
And that of others.   The great din ye heard
Foreshadows crack of doom—You all shall
   die
Ere many days.   The weapons that ye saw
Mean battle imminent and terrible.
The croaking ravens with the iron beaks,
They are the devils and the heathen gods
In whom ye trust ;   they shall drag down
   your souls

Deep into Hell.'' Then Brodar was so wroth
He spoke no word at all, but left the ship,
And going to his men he bade them range
Their vessels 'thwart the harbour-mouth,
    and chain
Each to the other and to either shore,
That we could not escape. But in the night
We lifted anchor, and with long poles pushed
Along the shore and cut his cables through.
Then was confusion among Brodar's ships;
They fell afoul, colliding in the dark.
So all our galleys safely got to sea
And turning west to Ireland, we laid course
Round the south coast; and now, a league
    away,
Our ships lie safe upon the Shannon's tide;
Five hundred men I have—all warriors tried;
They too would Christians be and all enlist
Under your flag to fight your enemies.
This is my tale, O King!

King Brian :—
A wondrous tale
And one in which I see the hand of God.
Thou art thrice welcome, Ospak, to our ranks,
And honour and distinction shall be thine.
But now I ask a question, which if thou
Canst answer, thou shalt do us service vast;
In this great enterprise we have at heart—:
Did Brodar tell thee where the Viking fleet
Would make combined attack?

Ospak :—
Oh, gentle king,
Glad is my heart that I can answer true:
The Vikings munster all in Dublin Bay.
A week before the holy Feast of Palms

King Brian :—
'Tis well, my friend, thou sure art sent of
    God.
At Dublin ere the Feast of Palms shall stand
Our armies trained and ready.

[*To other Kings*]—
You have heard
Your question answered, as it were from
    heaven.
Doubt not that Christ is on His people's side.
His plundered shrines and burned sanctuaries
Have cried to him for vengeance on the Dane.
Go ye then forth and bring your clansmen here
In war-array. But, ere you sally out,
Hearken MacLiag's song.
Our bard has notes
That light the battle-fire in warrior-souls.
MacLiag :—
Puissant king
I sing of Brian marching 'gainst his foes :—
        [*Strikes the harp and sings.*]
I hear the Crow of Battle,
    That croaks above the Slain ;
The howling war-wolves gather,
    They scent a gory rain.
Athwart the sable heavens
    Staggers a blood-red star.
Men veil their eyes in mortal fear,
Deep groaning of the dead I hear,
And hark, that trumpet screaming near ! •
    King Brian goes to war !

Ghosts of our ancient heroes
    Loom thro' the misty air ;
The eyes of Finn and Conall
    With wild exulting glare.
Spear-poising, great Cuchulain
    Sweeps past in scythed car ;
Conn of the Hundred Fights is there,
And Oscar of the raven hair,
While god-like Naesi, nobly fair,
    With Brian goes to war !

In the walled cities meeting
    The pagan pirates cower,

Their demon-gods entreating
  Against the fates that lower.
Their sins cry out for vengence
  At Heaven's justice-bar.
Dark doom shall whelm them, for they took
'Chalice and pyx and sacred book,
And on their chastening men shall look
  When Brian goes to war!

Then forward, chiefs and leaders!
  Forward the rank and file!
Our lives we gladly offer
  To save this sainted Isle;
That Sun-burst blazing o'er us
  No coward deeds shall mar;
For Christ shall fight for us this day,
And Holy Mary for us pray,
And Patrick all our foes affray,
  When Brian goes to war!
  [*All applaud.*]

King Brian :—
  It is well sung, MacLiag. By St. Bride
  No king had ever truer bard than I!
  And there is this thou hast reminded me :—
  God's blessing shall be needed on this work,
  God's and His Church's; for the mightiest
    king
  Without that blessing is more mean and weak
  Than the most wretched slave. For what is
    power
  But a free gift from Him, and to be used
  For His great glory Who has made the world?
  Therefore, Lord Bishop, now behold us kneel
  For Heaven's blessing on our enterprise.
[*All kneel. Fridolin, the Bishop, advances,
and, making the Sign of the Cross over them three
times, says :*]
Fridolin :—
  I bless you, chiefs and soldiers, in the Name

Of Christ Who triumphed over sin and death;
I bless you in the Holy name of Mary,
Who loves our Isle, and will protect its
    shrines ;
I bless you in the pow'rful name of Patrick,
Who made this Island Christian, and will drive
The pagan wolves away.   I bless you now
In Columkill's and holy Brigid's names—
Saints of the Gael.   Soldiers, go forward all
In fervent faith and fearless constancy
To battle for your altars and your homes !
[*All rise and go out.   The curtain falls.*]

ACT II.—SCENE I.

[*The Sea Coast.*]

[*The Princess Reinalt and her handmaiden,
Nuala, are seen seated on a ledge of rock.   Beside
them a great cape juts out into the sea, and hides a
small harbour on the other side from their view.*]

Reinalt :—
    How beautiful this world appears, which God
    Has given to us to be our very own !
    Yet, how ungrateful are we—we neglect
    To praise His goodness ;   and by sin we mock
    The Blood that flows from Jesus' sacred
        wounds
    Which opened for our sake, so that we might
    Not die eternally,   Ah, Nuala,
    Often at hours like this there comes the
        thought
    To leave the world, and all it promises
    Of wealth and glory and of happiness—
    For these things as a princess may be mine—
    To leave them all for our dear Saviour's sake.
    He hath giv'n all for us, and shall we not
    Make sacrifice for Him ?

Nuala :—

My mistress sweet,
Such thoughts are wholesome for thy gener-
    ous soul ;
Yet, it may be God's will that such a course
Is not for thee.   Thrice blessed those happy
    ones
Who in the cloister seek the only peace—
The peace of God ;   but there are many more
Who in the world must witness unto Christ
And bear His yoke. The House of Brian needs,
In order to the safety of the land
And to its future weal, alliance with
The kings of the Hy Niall in the North ;
And it is known that ere this coming fight
Unto the Tanist thou wilt be betrothed.
With such a union of the north and south
Our Holy Church need never fear again
The Viking spoilers.   What a noble part
Is thine in saving our dear land from ill
And all our shrines from plunder !

Reinalt :—

As to this
I shall consult good Bishop Fridolin,
And be advised by him.   My heart is free
And I could learn to cherish and to love
The Prince O'Neill, of whom I have heard tale
That he is tall and brave.   Now dearest
    friend,
Sing me a song of Erin's olden days,
And of the heroes bold, and ladies fair,
Who dwelt therein.   Last night the harper
    sang
Some strange old ranns of beauty and of grief
That have bewitched my soul.   And after-
    wards
I dreamt I stood on a wild mountainside
And heard the golden sound of the Dord
    Fiann

Finn's hunting horn, and then a deer
   rushed by—
Followed by Finn and all his noble train !
Pale Oscar and Oiseen I noticed there,
And Diarmuid of the Love-spot.   All did
   gaze
Upon me with such wistful yearning look
My heart was melting.   As I hurried down
The mountain side I met a reverend man,
Grave and white-bearded ; whom I ques-
   tioned :
" Why are the Finian chiefs thus sorrowful ?"
And smiling kindly he made answer thus :—
" Oh, maiden of great Eire's royal line,
The Finians are sad because they see
King Brian setting out to glorious war
Without their company.   To them more sweet
The sound of shield 'gainst shield, and sword
   on helm,
The roar of warriors in combat locked,
Than all the gentle pleasures of the chase ! "
And then I woke.   So, sing me of the Past.

Nuala :—
   Loved Princess, 'tis my pleasure to obey
     (*Sings*)—

I am mourning for Conhor the king, without peer
   in Ierne ;
Straight-limbed and tall as the birches that
   wave by Loch Inver ;
The King whom we followed to battle, like young
   gods rejoicing,
His yellow hair streaming before us, a meteor
   fitful,
I mourn now for Conhor the King.

I am mourning for Lasair, the queen, most
   majestic of women ;
Brow-bound, with jewels, broad-zoned with the
   silver of Saimer,

Sweet-voiced, and lavish of gifts to the war-
  spent battalions !
Bearing us food, and kind welcome from ·foray
  and battle !
    I mourn now for Lasair the queen.

I mourn now for Deirdre the Beautiful—saddest
  of women ;
With tresses that shone like gold torques on a
  snow-covered hillock !
Naesi and Ainnle and Arden, first flowers of
  knighthood,
Died for her gladly, while all the Red Branch
  wailed in sorrow.
    I mourn now for Deirdre the Fair.

I mourn for the days that are dead—ere my youth
  had evanished ;
The high mountained played with me then, and
  the loud shouting tempest
To me was a brother in strength ; the wild roar
  of the torrent
But lulled me to sleep—now I long for the sleep
  with no waking—
    I mourn for the days that are dead.

[*While the song is being sung, a Viking ship
slips into the little cove beyond the cliff, and there
warriors land. Unseen, in the shelter of the
boulders, they listen to the singing, and at the last
note rush in upon the maidens, and bind their
hands behind their backs. They are about to
drag them away, when the leader of the Vikings
a tall, handsome youth, clad in complete armour,
and with a naked sword in his hand, appears upon
the scene. For a moment he gazes in astonish-
ment upon the scene, then he utters a sharp command,
and the pirates precipitately release their prey.*]

Leader :—

> How now, you dogs ? What were my orders
>   late ?
> Bold, Thorkel, Grimm, what deviltry is this ?
> Did I not warn you that upon these coasts
> Where the good monarch Brian holdeth sway,
> No injuries be done ? Are your fierce hearts
> So prone to crime and violence, that even
> My strict commands and wishes go for nought,
> By Thor and Odin, but these maids are here
> Unused to deeds of blood and violence,
> I'd prove upon ye with this trusty sword
> That Thorstein, son of Hall, must be obeyed
> Even to the letter. Get ye to the ship,
> And thank the Norns ye go with little scathe!

*[The three Vikings hurry to the galley with every
appearance of fear, Prince Thorstein regarding
them with lowering looks as they go. He then
turns to the maidens, and unties their hands.]*

Thorstein (addressing Reinalt) :—

> Gentle fair Princess,—for I know the signs
> Of royal rank and blood—I crave thy pardon
> And that of thy companion, for the rude
> Unseemly conduct of these knaves of mine.
> Had they but hurst a hair upon your heads
> Their life had paid the forfeit. Even now
> Say but the word and all the three shall die!

Reinalt :—

> Noble Prince Thorstein, we are Christian
>   maids,
> And would forgive, even were our blood
>   out-poured.
> Spare then these thoughtless ones, and for
>   thine act
> Of timely mercy please accept our thanks
> And boundless gratitude.

Thorstein :—
  Oh, Princess fair,
  Tell me thy name that I may ever keep
  Its letters in my heart; for thy sweet face
  Shall follow me upon the billows wild.

Reinalt :—
  I am called Reinalt, grand-daughter of Brian
  And daughter of Prince Murrough.   Wouldst
    thou come
  With us unto the court, a meet reward
  The King will give thee.

Thorstein :—
  Dearest maid, no king
  Could give reward that equals thy sweet looks
  And friendly words.   Besides, I must not risk
  Detention here, till the dispute be fought
  Betwixt the races.   Thorstein must be there
  In danger with his brothers.   When this fight,
  Which shall be waged for winning of the
    world,
  Is done—if yet I live—I will come back,
  And now, farewell! farewell!

[*He bows and goes, turning back to look again
ere he disappears behind the cliff.*]

Reinalt :—
  Sweet Nuala, what strange adventure this!
  There goes a warrior that I could love—
  So graceful, brave, and manly.   Much I fear
  That I have given him my maiden heart.

Nuala :—
  He almost has mine, too—but what a fate
  It were to love a Viking of the deep,
  Lawless and cruel—tossed from shore to shore
  By the mad seas, and chased by ruthless foes!
  I'll love no Viking! and for thee, Princess,
  There is the marriage with the great O'Neill;
  Forget it not.

Reinalt :—
And If I did forget,
Thou'dst soon recall it.

[*She turns and gazes sadly and wistfully over
the ocean*].

Lo, I see his ship
Framed in the setting sun that throbs and
   glows
In pulsing colours round it. So, alas,
His imaged face is framed within my soul.
I'll pray to Mary, God's elected Mother
That she may bring this sea-prince unto
   Christ,
Or aid me to forget.   Who cometh now—
This giant warrior clad in battle-mail
With sword unsheathed ? Why, 'tis Kerthial
My noble cousin, bravest of the brave.
How now, great Kerthial ? Wherefore goest
   thou
With such an eager and an anxious look ?

Kerthial :—
There was some rumour of a Viking ship,
And so I came to bring the ladies home.

Reinalt :—
Oh, tardy Kerthial, we had been lost
But that a fairy prince came from the sea
And rescued us!

[*Takes his hand in hers.*]

Dear cousin Kerthial,
In the great battle that is soon to be
If thou should'st meet a noble chief, by name
Of Thorstein, son of Hall, spare thou his life
And bring him here to me.

Kerthial :—
An' if I have
To ring his nose, and lead him with a rope,
I'll bring him to thee ! So my little maid

Doth favour Vikings ! Only say the word
I'll hale thee a round dozen from the wars—
Baresarkers all, with glassy eyes like dolls
And hair on fire !
Reinalt :—
Impetuous Kerthial!
If thou dost bring the one that I have named
Thou shalt have praise enough. Put u
    thy sword
And lead us homeward ere the darkness fall.
[*Exeunt.*]

SCENE II.

[*The great banquet hall of Earl Sigurd at Hrossey
in the Orkneys. Sitric, King of Dublin, is the
guest of honour. Beside him sit Earl Sigurd
and Earl Gilli of the Southern Isles. Next to Earl
Sigurd sits Prince Thorstein, the son of Hall of
The Side. Around the board are many Vikings
from Iceland who had lately taken part in the
celebrated burning of Njal, the great Icelantic
law-giver; which incident gave name to the
immortal " Saga of Burnt Njal." Their leader's
name is Flosi. Some of the others are :—Hroar of
Hromunstede ; Gunnar Lambi's son the Skald ;
Ingialld of the Springs ; Sigmund Sigfus' son ;
Thorstein Broadpaunch's son, Kel ; Glum, the
son of Hilldir, and Thord, the son of Illugi of
Mauratongue.*]

Earl Sigurd :—
Now tell us, Flosi, of this luckless feud
That ended in the burning up of Njal
Iceland's wise law-giver. What of his son
Helgi, that was a henchman of mine own ?
Flosi :—
The last I saw of Helgi was the time
I cut his head off with a mighty blow
Outside the burning house of Bergthorasknoll

Earl Sigurd :—
　By Thor and Odin 'twas an evil deed!
　I may be forced to vengeance for it yet.
　But tell us more about that monstrous crime.
Flosi :—
　We have here Gunnar, Lambi's son, a Skald
　Let him now sing the end of Burnt Njal.

[*As Gunnar stands up to sing, three other Vikings
enter the room. They are Kari and Kolbein, and
David the White. Kari is the sworn comrade of
Skarpedin the son of Njal, and all three are
partisans of the dead law-giver.*]

Gunnar :—
　Flosi and his band came rushing
　'Gainst the house of Bergthorasknoll ;
　Skarpedin and Grim and Helgi
　Flung out spears and stopped their course.
　Helgi Njal tried escaping ;
　Flosi's sword cut off his head.
　When they set the house a-burning
　Kari tossed out blazing brands.
　Njal and Bergthora burned,
　And within their arms expired
　Thord, the little son of Kari.
　Kari leaped through flame and smoke,
　Reaching safety unnoticed.
　Skarpadin was trapped by falling
　Of the beams above his head ;
　Long time he had battled bravely,
　Then he wept with pain and fear—!
Earl Sigurd :—
　Did Skarpedin show fear and cowardice ?
　I scarce can credit it !
[*Kari advancing with drawn sword*] :—
　'Tis a black lie
　Skarpedin never quailed—He knew not fear.
[*Kari attacks Gunnar who retreats behind the*

arras. They fight, and with a great blow of Kari's sword the head of Gunnar is severed from his body. The head by force of the blow bounds over the curtains, and lands on the table in the midst of the feast. The table, and the clothes of Earl Sigurd, are splashed with blood.]

Earl Sigurd :—
  Seize Kari, now, and kill him where he
    stands !

[*All stand up, but no one attempts to seize him.*]
Kari :—
  Earl Sigurd, there are many who would say
  That I have done you service by this deed,
  Avenging Helgi, Njal's son, your friend.
Flosi :—
  Let Kari go, he owes us no atonement,
  And hath not done this deed without a cause.

[*Kari goes out to his ship, and his comrades with him. The table is cleansed from gore, and the dead body is borne away.*]

King Sitric :—
  That was a mighty fellow, and a bold
  Who stoutly dealt that stroke, not thinking
    twice !
Earl Sigurd :—
  There is no man like Kari, in the North,
  For dash and daring and a sudden stroke.
  But tell us now the purpose that hath brought
  Thee to our Court, and we will listen well.
King Sitric :—
  Ere now, Earl Sigurd, had not these hot broils
  Disturbed our conversation, I had told
  The gist and reason of my visit here ;
  'Tis this in brief : A powerful league is
    formed
  Of all the Scanian Race against King Brian ;
  We have resolved the Raven-Flag shall float

O'er all the land of Erin.　This to join
Thou art invited—all the ties of blood
And race and country call on thee to aid
This vast confederacy of Viking strength.
Shall I not have thy hand on it?

Earl Sigurd :—
Not so!
I must consider.　War I like full well;
But war against so good a king as Brian,
I like it not!　What think ye, all my men?
Shall we attack King Brian—Yea or Nay?

Soldiers (*loudly*) :—
Nay, nay,—no war with Ireland's noble king!

Earl Sigurd :—
Thou seest that my soldiers look on Brian
As one to reverence, not to war against.
Besides, the chances of success are slight
Unless the Vikings gather in great force.
What is their muster-roll?

King Sitric :—
'Tis great and vast;
Donat and Conmael, sons of Denmark's king,
And Olaf Prince of Lochlan will be there
With many thousands clad in shining mail.
Brodar with all his galleys comes from Man,
And Vikings from an hundred island coasts,
From the deep fjords, and from the German
　bays—
Never was muster like it seen before,
And rich shall be the plunder!　Shalt thou
　roost
Here on thy barren rocks, like blinking owl,
While all those splendid ospreys of the sea
Swoop on their prey?

Earl Sigurd :—
Aye, but the gallant Brian
Will make no easy picking!　Should I go
I must have surety that, if we win,
Sigurd, the son of Hlodver—even I—

Shall be made king of all the conquered realm,
And Gormly, the fairest of all women,
Must be my queen.

King Sitric :—
Upon my solemn word
Of honour, as a prince unto a prince,
Thou shalt have this and more.

Earl Sigurd :—
'Tis settled, then,
My ships and men shall join this Viking league
Where shall we meet?

King Sitric :—
The mustering of hosts
Will be at Dublin, on the Feast of Palms.
I see a prince of Iceland at the board
Him too I ask, with all his henchmen strong
To join with us,—Thorstein, son of Hall

Thorstein :—
I had resolved to join
The Viking hosts; not that I hate King Brian
Or love the carnage of the battlefield,
But that I see this fight will be the test
Of Viking manhood. Should we fail in this
Our race and blood are doomed; and so I go
To share the fate of all my kith and kin.

King Sitric :—
Farewell then, brothers, till the Feast of
    Palms,
And may the Norns still fructify our hopes !

[*Exeunt.*]

Scene III.

[*The Viking camp at Dublin Bay. Ben-Edair
(The Hill of Howth) and Ireland's Eye, are seen
in the distance. The whole Bay is covered with
Viking galleys. In front of a large tent are seated
in council, Queen Gormly, Mailmora, King of
Leinster ; Sitric, King of the Danes of Dublin ;
Brodar, Admiral of the Fleet ; Suibhne, Earl of*

Man ; Sigurd, Earl of Orkney ; Canuteson, Prince of Denmark ; Carlus and Anrud, Princes of Norway ; and Thorstein, Son of Hall of the Side, of Iceland.]

Queen Gormly :—
This grand array of all the Viking race
Eager for battle, is assurance good
That in the coming contest we shall curb
The insolence of Brian, and bring back
The pagan gods once more into this land.
For I am sick to death of Christian law
That curbs the bold and daring, and torments
The weary flesh with fasts and penances ;
Wherefore, I greet you gladly, noble kings,
And wish you glory in your enterprise.
The spoils of victory will be immense.
Fight well and stoutly ! It is known to
    me
And to my brother, King of Leinster, here,
That Brian hath sent many troops away,
The flower of his Dalcassian chivalry,
To ravage Leinster under Donough's lead ;
Wherefore I would advise that ere return
Of these battalions we should make attack
Good Friday morning on the Irish host.
What think ye, noble Vikings ?
Thorstein :—
Kings and chiefs,
I like it not, this shedding of much blood
On a great Christian feast. We have with us
Of Christian Vikings quite a numerous band,
Who do abhor to fight on such a day.
Bethink ye, is it wise to scorn the Christ
Who died that day, but rose again from death.
The Christian God is powerful, and oft
Hath humbled even Odin in the dust.
Brodar (scornfully) :—
To hear Prince Thorstein argue, one would
    think

That he were ripe to be a Christian, too,
Thorstein :—
    If ever I be Christian, I will not,
    Like Brodar, turn God's dastard, and recant,
Brodar :—
    Have care, have care, young braggart of the
      North,
    Thou goest too far to taunt me thus—this
      sword
    May teach thee manners!
Thorstein :—
    Come let's settle it
    Unsheathe and stand against me, or thou art
    The coward I have deemed thee!
King Sitric :—
    What! and shall
    Our captains quarrel ere the fight be won?
    For shame, I say; put up your angry swords!
    All Vikings must be brothers on this day,
    Or all our hopes are lost. Put up your
      swords!

[*Thorstein and Brodar put up their swords slowly and reluctantly, glaring at each other the while.*]

King Sitric :—
    In scanning now the faces of the chiefs
    I have remarked that all do throw their will,
    (Except the Prince of Iceland) to the side
    That would give battle on Good Friday morn.
    Wherefore, it seemeth best that I should ask
    If such be really their desire and wish,
    Shall we then fight on Friday when Christ
      died?

[*All the Viking chiefs, except Thorstein, shout: "Yes, yes,—Lead us against the foe!" Earl Sigurd stands up to speak and a great uproar of applause breaks out, and cries of " Let Sigurd lead us— Sigurd, Hlodver's son!"*]

Earl Sigurd :—
Princes and Chieftains! Since the die is cast
And battle ordered, let us bear ourselves
As valiant Norsemen worthy of our sires.
The god of battle, Odin, whom we serve
Will grant us triumph, if our cause be just.
Yet though we lose, if each but play his part
Like warrior brave, and die upon the field,
The Valkyries, the Choosers of the Slain
Will bear unto Valhalla, Odin's house
That warrior's soul. It is man's lot to die :
A gloomy fate inexorable hangs
Each day above his head. Man perishes ;
But noble fame, well earnè, never dies ;
So, since we may not destiny avoid,
Let us go forth and meet it like bold men
Under the Raven Banner that has flown
On misty seas o'er many dangerous fights.
On, Vikings ! On, for Odin's sacred cause !

[*All stand up and shout loudly :—"Odin and
Victory ! Odin and Victory ! "*]

[*Curtain.*]

ACT III.—SCENE I.

[*The Irish camp at Dublin. In the distance can
be seen the Danish army, the Viking ships on
Dublin Bay. In the foreground is the pavilion
of the Ard Righ, Brian, before which are seated the
High King himself, and many other kings and
chieftains, including Malachy: King of Meath ;
Ospak, the Dane ; The Great Stewards of Mar and
Lennox ; Brian's sons, the Princes Murrough,
Donald, Conhor, Flan and Teige ; the warrior
Kerthial ; Kian, son of Malloy ; Donal, son of
Dhu Davoren ; O'Kelly, Prince of Hy Manie ;
O'Heyne, King of Hy Fiachra Ahna ; Melmary,*

*King of Hy Liathan ;   Mothla, King of the Decies ;
and Echtigern, King of Dalaradia.*]

[*Time—The early morning before the Battle of
Clontarf.*]

King Brian :—
 Think ye the Vikings will attack to-day ?
 'Tis monstrous if they show irreverence
 By spilling blood upon the holy hour
 When Christ lay dying on a cross for men !
 I have sent message to their very camp
 Begging them to defer until next day
 The opening of conflict.   Are there here
 Who know of later tidings ?

Ospak :—
 Noble King,
 Not many minutes past, my soldiers took
 A Danish spy, who, on being put to pain,
 Told us that, some days gone, the sorcerers,
 By Brodar were consulted, and replied
 That if before Good Friday they gave fight,
 The Danes would lose.   But if upon that day
 Battle was joined, King Brian sure would fall.
 'Twas then resolved by common vote of all,
 That on the morning of that holy day
 They would attack in force.

King Brian :—
 'Twould thus appear
 There is no time to lose.   The right wing then
 Murrough and his brave brothers will
  command
 With Malachy of Meath,   Our central force
 Donal, the son of famed Dhu-Davoren,
 And Kian, worthy son of great Malloy
 Will lead to strife.   Our left will be brought on
 By the proud Princes of Connacia.
 King Echtigern will join with them.   May
  Christ
 Strengthen your souls when the deep dread
  of war

Falls down like midnight o'er the reddened
    field !
May Mary, His sweet Mother go before
Your blessèd banners, cheering all your hearts,
And welcoming to heaven all who die
In her good cause!   Remember, noble chiefs
And warriors tried, the issue of this day
Decides the fate of Erin.   Your strong line
Alone divides the Viking from his prey.
Should that line waver, all our lovely land—
Our bright, green vales, our mountains
    heather-crown'd,
Our lakes like crystal, and our thousand
    streams
Shall call the Pirate master.   Our far homes
And precious loved ones cry to us to-day
"Save us from sack and slaughter !"
                    Fearful thought—
Our shrines and churches, where we worship
    God,
And where He deigns to dwell—shall robber
    bands
Pillage and desecrate, extinguishing
Forever in this holy isle the light
By Patrick kindled ?   Think of future times,
The generations that are yet to come.
The holy saints, the priests, the men of God,
The missionaries whom this land shall send
To many foreign kingdoms, conquering
New countries and new peoples unto Christ !
Let us then crush to-day the Scanian hordes
And hurl them back forever in the seas !
Go forward, men of Erin, in Christ's Name,
Go forward without fear, and drag to earth
These Raven Banners that pollute the air
And darken all our skies !   Dalcassians brave,
Eugenians and Connacians worthy of
Your sires heroic, on to battle now,
And for the glory of the Triune God,
Drive Heathendom forever from our shore !

[*The King raises a Crucifix in his right hand,
and blesses all the army, making the Sign of the
Cross.*]

Look on this Sign ! On Calvary to-day
He died ; that Christian men might never fear
Pale Death, or Pagan power, or demon wiles !
Look on this Sign, and conquer in its light !

[*All the Chiefs cheer wildly, and rush to their
places crying out : "Christ and Victory ! Death to
the Heathen Vikings !"*]

SCENE II.

[SCENE—*The same, later in the day. King
Brian is seen kneeling in his tent, before a Crucifix.
Armed guards stand around eagerly watching the
battle, the din of which can easily be heard. Laiten,
a herald, unarmed, stands on a little mount in
front. The king comes forth and speaks to the
herald :—*]

King Brian :—
How goes the battle ?
Herald :—
At the first attack
The Danes were pushing back the Dalagais
When Murrough rushed against them
furiously,
And through the Viking ranks he made a
breach,
Cutting down fifty mail-clad warriors
To left and right ; for iron, hide, or bronze
Are soft to him alike, and such his strength
No man alive to-day can turn his blows !

[*The Herald is silent a while, gazing anxiously
ahead.*]

(*He speaks again*) :—
All, all is turmoil and confusion now ;
I scarce can know the Irish from the Danes ;
But there is stir where Kerthial's figure goes,
Like a strong whirlpool on a river-flood !

King Brian :—
    Tell me if Murrough's standard still doth
        wave ?
Laiten :—
    Murrough has passed it to the westward now
    But still it stands erect.
King Brian :—
    And while it stands
    All will go well with Erin's warriors ;
    For when they see that standard floating high
    Their strength and bravery return anew
    And with rejoicing hearts they front the foe.
[*The noise of the battle becomes louder and more
awful. The guards around the king of Ireland's
tent become excited, and forgetting their duty, many
of them rush off into the melee.*]
King Brian :—
    O Laiten of the eagle eye, how now
    Do Ireland's champions hold the ridge of war?
Laiten :—
    The field is now as if green Tomar's wood
    Were swept with fire, and all its underbush
    And slender trees had been cut down, and now
    Only the great boles stand. My eyes can see
    Only the strongest heroes left alive,
    And they are grimed with dust and clotted
        blood,
    While the confusion and the groaning sound
    As if the stones and wheels of some great mill
    Were turning all awry ! I see the Danes—
    The remnant left alive—being driven fast
    Into the red-stained sea. But Murrough's flag
    Is fallen, and I see it now no more.
King Brian :—
    The news you give is sad and joyful now ;
    The foreigner is driven from our shore,
    But Murrough, my brave son, is cold and dead !
    Alas, how can I live without my son,
    Erin's best knight ? My son ! my son !
        My son !

[*The last of the guards has rushed away to pursue the flying Danes.*]

Laiten :—

I see some people coming towards us now

King Brian :—

What do they seem like ?

Laiten :—

They seem shining blue, '
Or as stark naked, glittering in the sun.

King Brian :—

The people that you see are armoured Danes
And mean us harm.˺ Where have our sentries
    flown ?

[*The aged Ard Righ goes into the tent, and kneels to pray. Brodar and some Danes are passing hurriedly, when one of the latter who had once been in the Irish King's service recognizes the Monarch of Ireland.*]

Dane :—

That is the King of Ireland in the tent.

Brodar :—

'Tis not the king—'Tis but a Christian priest.

Dane :—

It is the King. It is the great King Brian,
    I know him well.

Brodar :—

He dies, if king or priest !

[*Brodar rushes at King Brian. His first stroke severs the arm of Laiten interposed. The Viking's second stroke is parried by the King who has drawn his sword. Brodar's next stroke cuts off the King's head. Brodar then appears outside the tent, grasping King Brian's head in his hand, and shouting aloud.*]

Let all men tell that Brodar felled great Brian

SCENE III.

[*A part of the field where the battle is raging. On the Irish side Kerthial is seen, leading the fight, The Raven Banner is there, with Earl Sigurd.*

Prince Thorstein, Hraft the Red, Asmund the White,
Erling of Straumay, and other Vikings around it.
Kerthial breaks through, and slays three successive
bearers of the Banner. Then Earl Sigurd shouts—]

Bear thou the banner, Thorstein, Son of Hall.
Asmund the White :—
Bear not the Banner! All who bear it die.
Thorstein (to Sigurd) :—
Bear thine own crow thyself, I'll touch it not.
Erling of Straumay :—
Thou dost well not to touch it. I had three
Fair, noble sons, who bore it—all are dead.
Earl Sigurd :—
Hrafn the Red, bear thou the banner, then.
Hrafn :—
I will not bear it, for it kills its friends,
It is accursed,   Bear thine own devil thyself !
Earl Sigurd :—
Yes, it is fit the beggar bear the bag.

[He tears off the flag and ties it around his body.
A moment afterwards he is pierced through with
a spear and dies.]

[The tide of battle surges to the left; a panic
seizes the Danes. They rush in wide-eyed terror
from the field, Prince Thorstein, who disdains
to fly, is borne back a space by the others ; but
frees himself, and scornfully bends down to tie
his buskin string. Kerthia, a terrible gore-splashed
figure, at the head of the pursuring Dalcassians
comes upon him in this act. He and his men are
thunderstruck with astonishment at the brave and
nonchalant bearing of the young Viking.]

Kerthial :—
How now, O Dane ! you run not like the
rest ?
Thorstein (smiling) :—
I run not, for 'tis foolishness to run ;

I can't get home to-night—my home is far
In distant Iceland 'mid the Northern seas.
Kerthial :—
You run not like the others ! Know you not
That at this moment I shall give you death
With one swift blow, as you are kneeling here.
[*Thorstein stands up, unarmed, and proudly
faces Kerthial.*]
Thorstein :—
Strike if you will. I fear not you or death ;
I have fought strongly in a losing cause ;
My kin are dead or scattered, and I see
A night of darkness closing o'er my race.
Kill me—I fear not you, and welcome death !
Kerthial :—
I do not wish to kill you, though we've sworn
To show no Viking mercy on this day.
What is your name, Oh, youth of fearless soul ?
Thorstein :—
My name is Thorstein ; I am son of Hall
Called " Of the Side," in the Icelandic tongue.
*Kerthial (embracing the Viking, and laughing
delightedly) :—*
So you are Thorstein ! Never have I seen
Such boldness and such bravery before
Upon a battlefield ! Sure, I might know
My little cousin Reinalt would have picked
A man that was a man ! I promised her
I'd take you home, and bring you to her door
If that I had to lead you with a rope.
How, now, Prince Thorstein, shall I need the
rope
Or will you come without it ?
Thorstein (smiling) :—
I will come
Without the rope, and glad of life again.
Kerthial :—
Give me your hand then, you are, too,
my cousin.
[*They go off, hand in hand. The curtain falls.*]

ACT IV.—SCENE I.

[*The throne room at Kincora. Prince Donough is seated upon his father's throne. Kerthial, Prince Thorstein, and many of the Dalcassian and Eugenian captains are standing around. The Princess Reinalt and her attendants are seen seated below the throne, and MacLiag the Bard leans dejectedly on his harp.*]

Prince Donough :—

I see, MacLiag, thou art deeply sad,
And broodest o'er the trials we have met
In the late battle. Who shall estimate
The loss to us and Erin of great Brian,
And all my noble brothers that have died
And left us desolate ? Yet, when we think
They gave their lives for God and for their
    land,
Surely their deaths are to be envied them !

MacLiag :—

I mourn for Murrough ; bitter tears I shed
For him, the torch of valour of the Gael,
Whose smile was like the breaking of the
    morn,
Whose frown was fear and death to Erin's foes.
Never was great Cuchulain, in the fight,
Greater than Murrough, when his sword
    mowed down
The mail-clad Norseman. Long their Skalds
    will sing
His peerless fame, who laid their leaders low !

Donough :—

Dwell not upon these griefs ; bethink thee
    now
Of Vikings routed from our sainted Isle,
And all the glory of the Faith restored.

MacLiag :—

I thank my God for all. Yet must I weep
For Teig and Donald, Conhor and tall Flann—
Heroes more comely than fair Usna's sons !
I mourn for Turlough of the yellow hair—

The tender son of Murrough. How the boy
Loved me and my old harp, and sat for hours
Listening to ranns about the Finians
And the Red Branch, and all the ancient
    tales !
How his blue eyes would blaze to emulate
The deads of Erin's champions, or again
The tears came welling softly when I sang
Of Naesi's death and Deirdre's sad lament !
Donough :—
Yet there were deeds performè at Clontarf
Which well deserve a harper's triumph song ;
And think of that great wonder at Ath-Ae
When all the wounded of the Dalagais
Entreated, and were tied to upright stakes,
With weapons in their hands to fight the foe !
No nobler heroes ever lived of old.

[*MacLiag strikes the harp, and sings :—*]

I cannot sing your hymns of victory ;
There comes a flood of sorrow to mine eyes,
Mine ears are stunned with Viking battle cries,
And by the margin of a blood-red sea
        King Brian martyred lies.

I see a strand with warrior corses strewn,
The salt waves washing in among the slain ;
Murrough is there, and Teig and Flann have lain
With Conhor and with Donald since the moon
        When Brian died in pain.

I hear the sea-wolves yelp in baffled rage,
The shouts of " Odin " linger on the air ;
On Tolka's wave young Turlough's yellow hair
Floats where the boy a fatal fight did wage
        'Neath Brian's dead cold stare.

Sweet Christ in Heaven, oh, aid me or I fall
In the red depths of madness and despair !
How can I live, and Murrough mouldering there,
While hid forever under Death's dark pall
        Lies Brian, loved of all ?

Donough :—
 I blame thee not, MacLiag, for thy gloom
 And bitter grief for our beloved dead ;
 Yet say I : they are happier being dead;
 For they have saved the Church ; and many
  a Mass
 Shall now be chanted for their favoured souls,
 And many a noble shrine and abbey fair
 Shall yet be raised unto their memory here
 In this my kingdom
[He turns and addresses the Viking.]
 Thorstein, son of Hall,
 Art thou resolved, as lately I have heard,
 To come to Christ, and leave the heathen
  gods ?
 If this be so, brave prince, whom now we call
 The "Death-Contemner," such an act of thine
 Shall gladden us beyond all golden gift.
Thorstein :—
 I am resolved, and long have been of mind
 To be a Christian.   All the Viking gods
 Are but the shadows of their wintry hills,
 Or cruel voices of the northern winds.
 I follow Christ, and take Him for my God.
Prince Donough :—
 'Tis well, my noble Thorstein ; this same
  night
 The Bishop, Fridolin, will thee baptize,
 Anointing thee into the Church of Christ.
 'Till then farewell, and angels be thy guard !

[Exeunt omnes.]

SCENE II.

*[A large room in the Palace at Kincora.   The
Princess Reinalt is seen, seated, and dressed as a
bride. Nuala, her handmaiden, is sitting near on
a low stool holding on her knee a small cruith,
or harp.]*

Reinalt :—
> It is my wedding day, and soon he comes
> To lead me to the Altar.   May sweet Christ
> Make me all worthy of Prince Thorstein's love,
> And Mary bless our union, that we live
> All sinlessly and holy in His sight.
> Dear Nuala, shall we not have a song
> To while away the hour ?

Nuala :—
> I know a lay
> That sings the requiem of the ancient gods.

[Nuala takes up the harp and sings.]

The pagan gods are doomed—in Erin now
Reigns the sweet, gentle Son, Who died for man ;
> The old war-burdened lays
> Give place to hymns of praise,
The psaltery of Christ drowns out the Druid rann.

Midhir and Lugh are shadows of the hills ; ,
Grey Mananan has stalled his demon steeds ;
> Young Angus and Etain,
> Long in the mould have lain,
And Aoivell in his shroud no mortal whisper heeds.

Deep in their caves of gold the Fairy Race,
The Sons of Dana, wait the Judgment Day ;
> Then shall they call on Him
> Who made their glories dim,
That He restore their heaven, for pride **long**
snatched away.

Balor and Bres are doomed—they walk **no more**
On Almhuin or on purple Sliabh-na-mban.
> The Viking hosts are flown
> From Toomhoon and Idrone,
For Odin follows fast where all the gods have gone.

Reinalt :—
> 'Tis beautifully sung, sweet Nuala
> Now talk to me of Thorstein, son of Hall !

Nuala :—
> Ah, there's a subject on which I can say

A hundred thousand things, and each one
  good.
Thou art indeed a princess favoured high
Above all Erin's daughters, that to-day
Thou marriest him—a paragon of men,
So like Cuchulain, or some youthful god;
Handsome as Angus Og, whom all the birds
Followed, and sang for very joy to see!
Lucky art thou, O princess, that O'Neill,
Though thrice commanded, sent no war-like
  aid
To Brian at Clontarf—for Donough now—
Who in the coming week will be made king—
Has vowed to chasten the rebellious North,
And thy betrothal to the Tanist there
Declared invalid. That is how it comes
Thou art to wed to-day, and wed the Dane.
But let me speak of Thorstein. What a man!
He is beloved of all the warriors,
And worshipped by all women. Goes he out,
The children follow him along the street,
To play with him and hear his wonder tales
Of krakens, and of bears, and icy hills,
That float upon the sea! And stranger still,
When men are dying and the priest has giv'n
The last anointment and viaticum,
They call for Thorstein, and they hold his
  hand—
For Death, they say, comes there not half so
  fierce,
But mild and gentle, having fear of him
Who conquered Death upon the stricken
  field!

Reinalt :—
Can this be possible? I did not know
The war-tried vet'rans thus respected him.
Yet truly it was worthy of a god
To conquer panic as brave Thorstein did,
To turn and front the red Dalcassians,
Standing alone when all the North had fled

Howling for mercy to its pagan gods
Oh, Nuala, 'tis a picture I will hold
Within my soul forever! And to think
That Kerthial should be the warrior
To meet my Thorstein, and to bring him here
Safe from all harm! Surely God has heard
My feeble prayers, and far beyond my worth
Requited me. Here comes bold Kerthial

[*Kerthial enters, and kneeling kisses her hand.*]

Welcome, great warrior, welcome Kerthial!
But where is he, thy fast companion?
For all men say that thou and he are friends
So loving and devoted that the one
Goes not without the other.

Kerthial :—

Dost thou mean
Prince Thorstein, son of hall? I left him
now,
Prinking himself in all the airs and hues
Of latest fashion. He is sore in fear
That at the wedding thou shouldst see some
flaw
Or crease in his costume! I almost laughed
Before his face, to see him thus afraid
Of one small maid—he, who had lately scorned
An army drunk with slaughter, and had
joked
Beneath my lifted axe. Here comes he now
And he will answer, doubtless, for himself.

[*Prince Thorstein enters, and salutes the Princess
with a kiss.*]

Thorstein :—

My sweetest Reinalt, is it all a dream,
A heavenly transport from which presently
I shall awake to old unhappiness?
But lately on a gory field I stood,
And saw my people vanquished, and the gods
In whom I trusted flouted and defied;
All things grew dark around me as I supped
The bitter wine of anguish, till I called

On death to come and claim me.   Then came
    one
Who spoke thy name, and at its mentioning
A light broke on my soul.   To-day, I stand
The happiest of men, for I have now
Christ for my God—and He hath given me
    thee!   [*Curtain falls.*]

SCENE III.

[*The curtain rises just after the celebration of the
marriage of Prince Thorstein and Reinalt.   An
Altar with lighted candles is seen.   The Bishop
stands upon the Altar step, his hands raised in
blessing over the newly-married pair.   The mem-
bers of the Royal Household, and the Dalcassian
Chiefs are seen standing on either side.*]

(*Bishop Fridolin speaks*) :—
    Princes and Chiefs of Erin, you have seen
    The Church unite as one this worthy pair,
    And all have joyed to note their happiness ;
    O, may it be a blessed augury,
    Of future unity and peace and love,
    Among the peoples of this favoured Isle,
    That, standing steadfast, they may never fear
    Or foreign foe, or internecine strife !
    This island, formed by God within His seas.
    To be a Nation proud, inviolate,
    Let no man rend with fratricidal strife,
    That dulls out swords and gives the invader
        place !
    This day let us rejoice for victory
    And for the overthrow of Pagan power ;
    But, ere the jubilation doth begin,
    Turn to His Altar here whereon He dwells
    Forever with us, and let chant of praise
    Rise to His worship from adoring hearts !
[*All turn and stand before the Altar.   The
Te Deum is chanted.   The curtain falls.*]

THE END.

CPSIA information can be obtained
at www.ICGtesting.com
Printed in the USA
BVHW041722051118
532208BV00024B/4639/P